·m 8.2

D1460193

Class   M

Tunes You've Always Wanted To Play

Easy Classics for

flute

with Piano Accompaniment
Arranged by Jack Long

CHESTER MUSIC

(A division of Music Sales Limited)
8/9 Frith Street, London W1V 5TZ

This book © Copyright 1997 Chester Music
Order No. CH61291 ISBN 0-7119-6686-9
Music processed by Enigma Music Production Services
Cover design by Pemberton & Whitefoord
Printed in the United Kingdom by Caligraving Limited, Thetford, Norfolk

CONTENTS

GYMNOPÉDIE No. I

E. Satie

ANDANTE CANTABILE

from String Quartet Op.3 No.5

F. J. Haydn

Andante cantabile

MINUET

from Anna Magdalena's Notebook

J. S. Bach

MARCH OF THE MEN OF HARLECH

Alla marcia

poco stacc. e sempre marc.

Welsh Air

PLAISIR D'AMOUR

G. Martini

Moderato

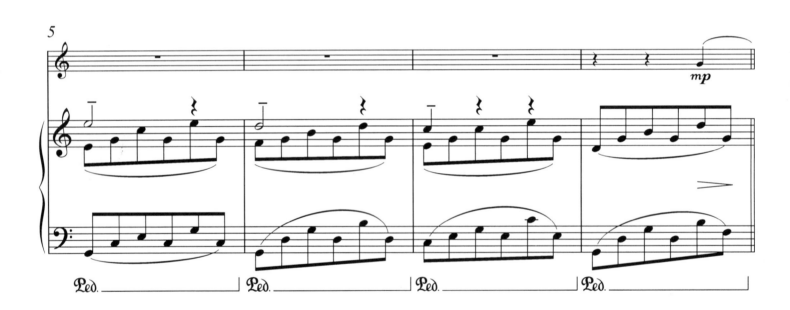

Ad lib. Ped.

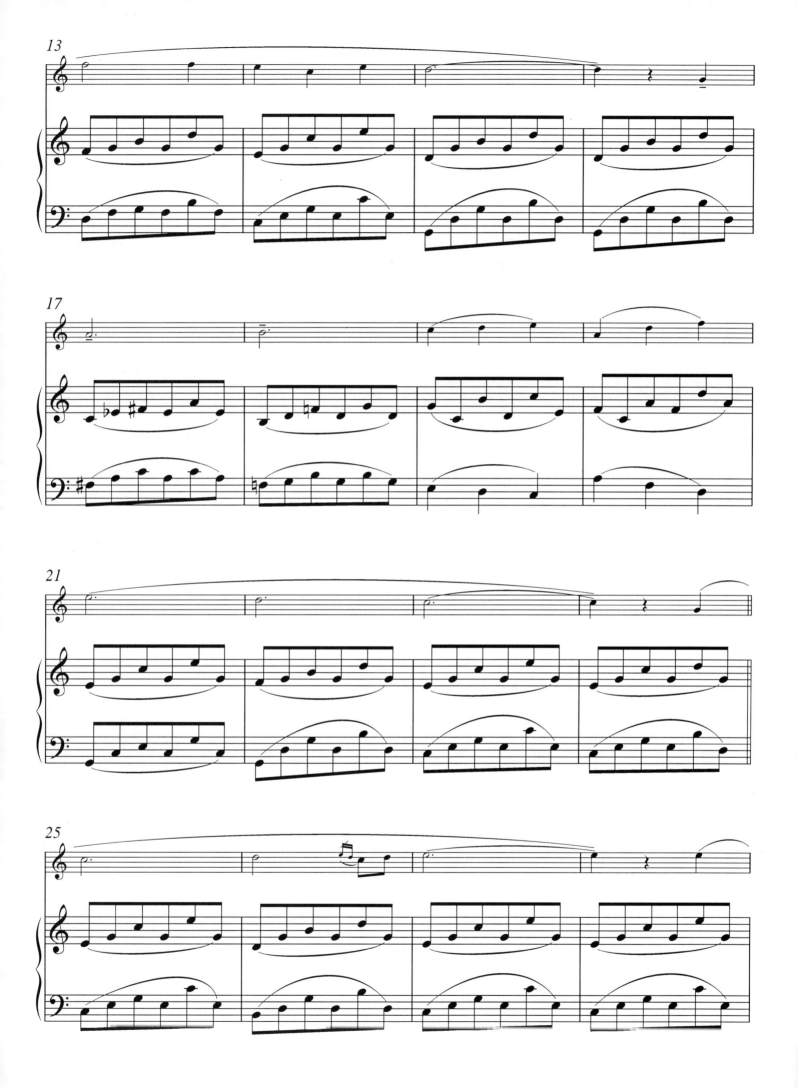

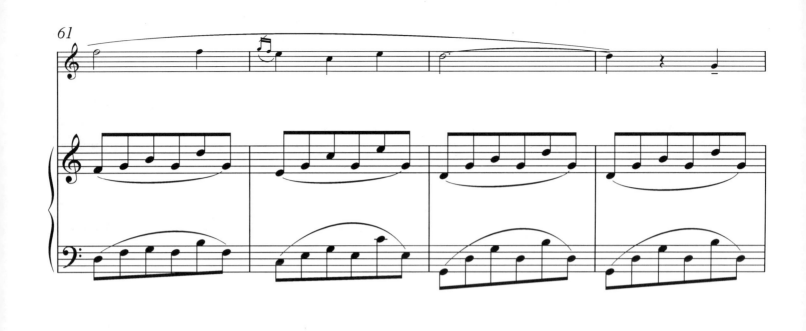

THE LONDONDERRY AIR

Irish Air

THEME FROM NEW WORLD SYMPHONY

Op. 95 2nd movement

A. Dvořák

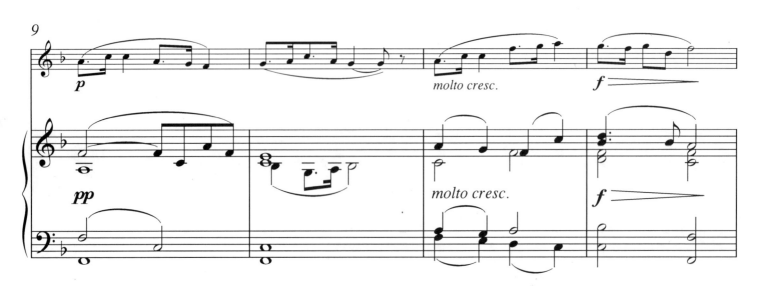

WHAT IS LIFE?

from Orfeo ed Euridice

C. W. Gluck

Andante espressivo

AIR ON THE G STRING

from Suite No.3 in D

J. S. Bach

Larghetto

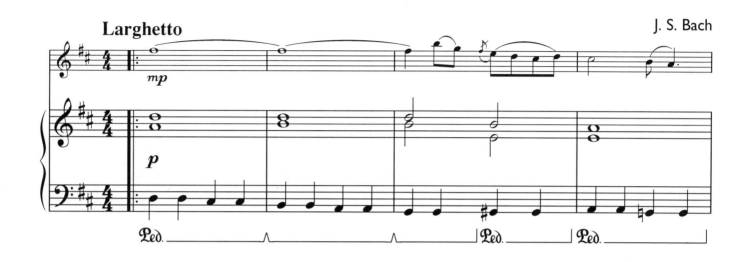

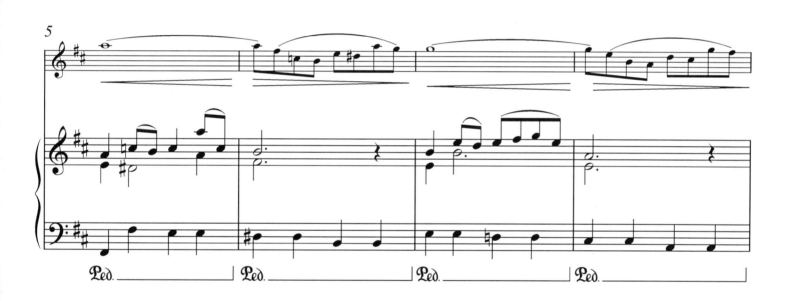

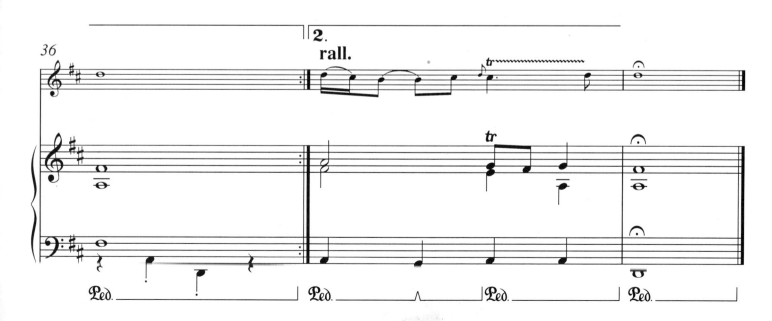

SCOTLAND THE BRAVE

Scottish Air

MINUET IN G

L. van Beethoven

Andante

AVE MARIA

Bach/Gounod

GREENSLEEVES/LOVELY JOAN

Andante sostenuto

English Airs

ANDANTE CANTABILE

from Quartet in D Op. 11

P. Tchaikovsky

Andante cantabile

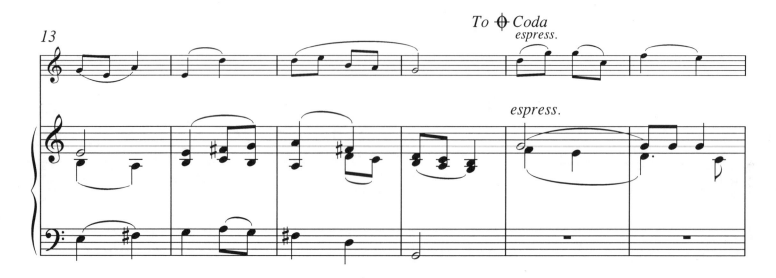

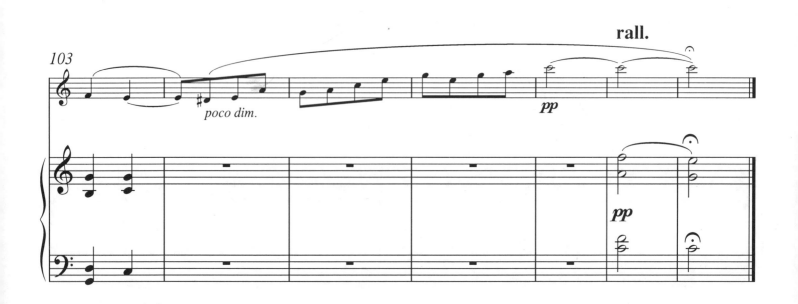

NOCTURNE

from Quartet No. 2 in D

Andante espressivo

A. Borodin

poco rall.

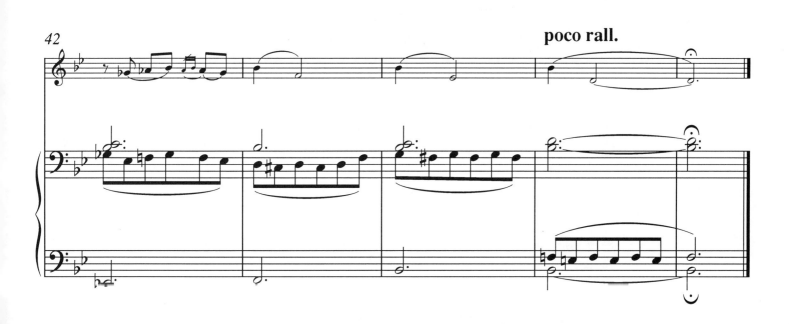

TRÄUMEREI

R. Schumann

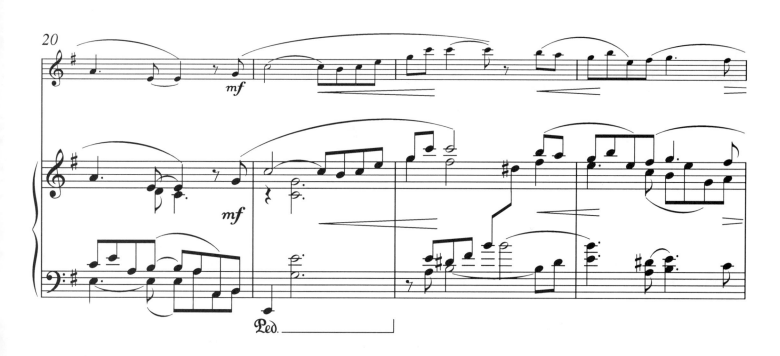

NORWEGIAN DANCE

Op. 35 No. 2

E. Grieg

Allegretto tranquillo

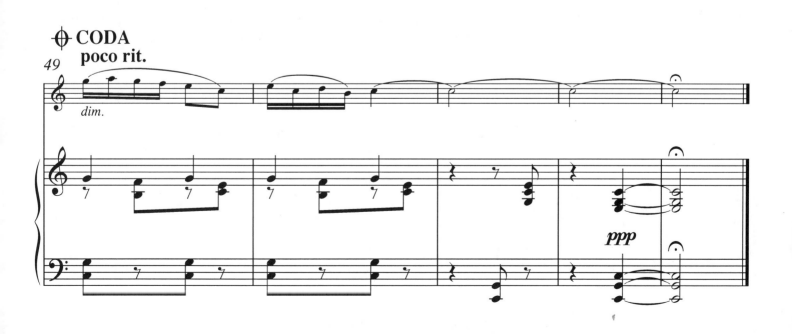

MINUET

Moderato e grazioso

L. Boccherini

BARCAROLLE

from Tales of Hoffmann

J. Offenbach

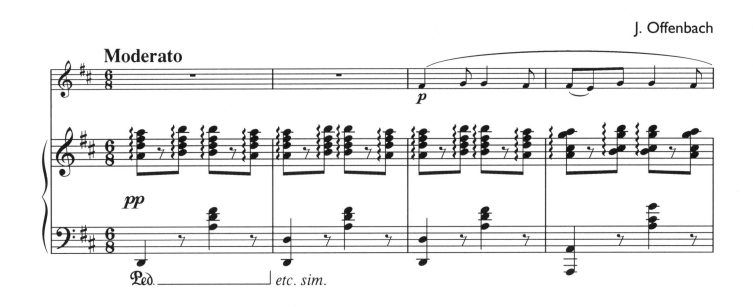

SPRING SONG
Songs Without Words, No. 30

F. Mendelssohn

Allegretto grazioso

FLOWER DUET

from Lakmé

L. Delibes

THEMES FROM EINE KLEINE NACHTMUSIK

W. A. Mozart

Allegro

11/99 (35870)